LONG SHADOW DAYS

GRIEF WALKING

Rick Wamer I Poems & Essays

A3D Impressions
Tucson I Minneapolis

A3D Impressions
P.O. 14181
Tucson, AZ 85732

Publisher's Cataloging-in-Publication data

Names: Warner, Rick, author.
Title: Long shadow days : grief walking / Rick Warner.
Description: "Poems and essays"--from cover. I Tucson, AZ;
Minneapolis, MN: A3D Impressions, 2022.
Identifiers: LCCN: 2022942086 I ISBN: 979-8-9864049-1-2
(hardcover) I 978-1-7344724-3-1 (paperback)
Subjects: LCSH American poetry--21st century. I Love--
Poetry. I Grief--Poetry. I Love poetry, American. I BISAC
POETRY / General I POETRY / Subjects & Themes / Death,
Grief, Loss I POETRY / Subjects & Themes / Love & Erotica
Classification: LCC PS3623.A73155 L66 2022 I
DDC 811.6--dc23

A3D Impressions
Tucson I Minneapolis

for Richard | Katherine Gloria | Kassie | Gloria | Theresa
and those they loved and who loved them

in loving memory of a dear friend and mentor, E. Reid
Gilbert, and my friend and fellow artist, Enrique Feldman

you live on within the excavations of my heart

acknowledgements

The following poems appeared in *Nature Inspired: Autumn:* Falling Leaves Press, Poughkeepsie, New York. 2016:

all the little losses
autumnal romance
in the hold of her embrace
ride on

Thank you, Christine Agro.

I would also like to thank all of life's losses for the teaching, in and through all of their manifestations.

contents

preface

It seems I've long embraced Grief as an ally in life, soothing the many losses along the way. I certainly recall very early and vivid sensations of the mystery of loss and death, as if veiled behind a scrim of almost, yet not, attainable knowing – palpable but untouchable. Grief, the process by which I confront this mystery, has long been befriended by me, and more often than I would wish, been enlisted to aid me in attending to losses, big or small.

This must have been apparent to others. Several decades ago, I spent a week in retreat, with a Spiritual Director originating from First Nations' heritage. Throughout the guided sessions for the retreatants, we shared our stories in a daily circle ceremony, based on prompts offered by the Retreat Master.

At the closing ritual session of the retreat, the Spiritual Director called us all into a celebratory naming ceremony whereby we were assigned a symbolic name to carry forward, based upon their impression they had of each of us and our shared stories. I recall being amazed and deeply moved by feeling a rich sense of being seen when they announced my ceremonial name, going forth – Grief Walker.

I still find deep meaning in this journey of life by walking beside Grief – inviting it in like a long-time companion who is there for me in times of loss.

Grief Walker! It seems I've long embraced Grief as an ally.

You hold in your hands a collection of works written in response to this experience of loss comforted by Grief, along with some lighter fare. After all, a Grief Walker we may all be, but life offers some consolations – even in their seeming brevity.

Reminded by the link between Grief and Loss, I came up with the collections title, Long Shadow Days. Winter light has also long been an important awareness for me, where the casting of great long shadows seems to be emblematic of those dark times of loss. Yet there is a glow that is particularly numinous in winter-shadow-cast light as if all the world is dressed in gold finery, the shadow a necessary companion in the revealing of nature's luminous beauty. The apparent link of the two seem parallel to my experience of Grief and Loss as ever constant companions.

May these small reflections, touch the shadows within your own life with illuminating light.

introduction

not so easy
grief arrives on the back of an unsuspected memory
stealing its way into my heart like a shroud eclipsing the day
my heart once again feeling stripped of all belonging

how is it that this frequent visitor comes
silent in approach
yet weighs so heavily in landing
anticipated coming always a surprise upon arrival

a familiar companion – sorrow
little time between visits

one has not time to welcome the guest
the meal must be served up
the plenty of the lost one's presence now gone
becomes the empty plate set waiting

ache decidedly has its temperaments
enthusiastic in its capacity
to call to heart the sensation of the beloved's walk
within the sojourn of communion laden days
then short tempered
irritable for the leaving
abandonment a powerful delusion

comes the contemplative pang
giving in to the gift grief bears in hidden ethers
gratitude
like the dissection of the fruit-seed of pomegranate
the preparations taken for a fine feast

across the temporal dimension of one's continuing
finally peace
the landscape of a lost one's leaving
the excavation that is now her presence
transformation the gift
loss the illusion
the excavation the lost one's receptacle

and the tears
oh the tears
the transporting vehicle to life's next landing

| •

Section I

Grief Walking

grief I

there is no leash
restrains it

there is no cage
contains it

resisting just
sustains it

befriending grief
though tames it

reluctant shores

stabbing pain of heartache's lament
unwelcome perennial guest upon my doorstep
how oft must I receive thee

longtime acquaintance by design not desire
reluctant playmates in the dance are we

awaiting your sure arrival
in waves of tears against my shores
lover of the sea must you be

life is a beautiful agony of unwanted sorrow

all these no-longer-with-me people
i've loved
the hands of time
cloak of death
the uncertain anxiety of parting lovers
afterglow
expended breathless passion
the way a fern unfolds
its green in the light of day
its passage brings the night
spring"s ever-present returning
first breath that sets the clockwork of our temporal existence
a burning candle
relentless persistence believing in love again
desiring my past in vain
a nagging wish to love with lasting desire
exuberant sunset opalescent moonrise
nighttime loneliness begs dawn to rise
a child's wonder and play
the distance i feel from my younger days
unending hope that nurtures through shadow and despair
the persistent edifice of dreams' broken remains
the memory of a kiss upon my lips
emblazoned fire within the soul and my belly
the way love transforms with the passage of time
knowing all of my wish-i-could-take-that-back mistakes
self-acceptance of all of my flawed facets of grace
the long unfolding

all ways grief walking
life is slow decay

may i speak of sorrow

days past when i lost, tears flowed with ease and grace,
my loss an experience to enter, sensations with meaning
... loss would leave me un-friended and i would rant, rave,
wallow in pain ... ascending from those depths exhilarated
in the cleansing, hopeful and energy bound; a sense of
adventure remained. Years on, now, sorrow is my
breathing, accepted companion as is the cycle of earth's
day

may i speak of sorrow

no rant no rave no pain
constant companion sorrow
guides acquiescence to her ways

i am not broken by her grip
nor loss's whip
i am enlightened by acceptance of grieving
which daily persists
such beautiful agony
recognizing the length of years ahead
briefer than those behind
beautiful agony not resisting loss

letting go

may i speak of longing

i so long to know endless love from a lover - love without end. i so long to be in my 20's again. i so long to feel the comfort that magical believing in a god once gave. i long to know my heart not jaded by years of self-knowing and the truths that living braves. i long to trust blindly again to risk all i am

i long to find joy in spring-breeze-blown drapery and drifting smells of garden summer savory. i long to hear neighborhood sounds of Good Humor making its rounds, while lying on my childhood bed, dancing patterns of light and shadow building daydreams in my head. i long to wonder at the new discovery rather than its rarity

i am grateful for my years, understand. i welcome the sum of any remaining. i am changed and changing. i am longing and light. i am sorrow and waiting. i journey still, through beautiful agony of unwanted sorrow while seeking her mystical delights, hoping, just hoping a few more days to borrow

baptism

loss
at once terrifying and beguiling
like peering over an unprotected precipice
eddies swirling below

letting go to the unwise impulse
leaping into air
thin
no buffering supports this stuff of breath
falling
falling through it
into the whirlpool of grieving
taken down to thick
down to thick black
down to thick black dark deep water
where even fish and plankton cannot find their stay

gulping
coughing and wheezing
erupting upon the surface
current swift
departing from emergence
yards now
no
miles away from the origins of my grieving
yet still within it

i float past new greenery not yet mine
waiting to greet the new world embracing me
leading me to I know not where

impossible to see the "through it of things"
i continue upon the flow
trusting the very waters that threaten my breathing

sealed in

under a glass dome
stepping stones
to tree umbrella canopy

granite floating upward
separated stones
spiraling each larger than the last

arriving atop the final stone
stem trunk broken
canopy in disarray

dark red clouded earth
and sky
my stone heart

what the fuck was i thinking

defending grief as an ally
what the fuck was I thinking
now death storms in with its icy toes
soiling the verdant earth of your traversals
changing earth to cold hard stone

my desire now for this broken heart

stone - not to feel
stone - not to know
stone - not to be left
in your fuck'n unknown

i demand Death's death

i want you to coffee jam with
to perform on stage with
to sandbox play with
to gourmet dine with
to fire pit drink with

stone breaks down – sand and earth again

not much choice
but to shelter
in the arms of Grief
after all

all the little losses

like pavement black
smooth clean
extending ubiquitous

we are laid upon the world
life's path unknown before us
inviting us to disembark

weather graces and perils the journey along the way
nature unpredictable in her stay
glorious sunsets here
then thunderous cyclones appear

as all things decay organic matter losing form
to reassemble anew obliquely foreseeable
we are broken down - identities lost
shaken by discombobulation upon the path

repaving the self resumes
like salvage of war-torn embattlement and edifice
yet with new knowing from all the little losses

remnants combine with insights anew
building yet the self
next to weather life's forces

i had forgotten

dwelling among specters of love lost
no longer held keepsakes
solitude surrounding alone

i had forgotten
as forgets the goblet
filled with grape's nectar
not anticipating its downing
empties again

i had forgotten
until the presence of your leaving
descended upon me
as though a cyclone
clean swept my soul of all belonging

vanishing foam

it is with a sense of sad elation
that i return home this eve of questioned tomorrows
your image echoing through the gray matter stuff of me

you are the source
the goddess
being of all beginnings

you are the infinite
the depth of nothing less than
the presence of "every"

i like rushing waves
crash upon your rocky shores
broken by the jagged edges of your apron

i am vanishing foam
fading from your beach
barely a crest line in the sand now

soon you will not even know me
my once rushing sign of passage through your days
now gone

and you there
dealing with the next wave
surrendering to your siren call

whimpering man

facing oblivion
i continue to wonder
why such pain
why lonely again

year upon year
the future to ponder
flash in a pan
this whimpering man

cacophony of stuff
are we just mass and matter
galactic gyre
or universal fire

drifting light
are we destined to scatter
a flaming dier
upon a funeral pyre

no more metaphors

sometimes it seems there are no more metaphors
similes packed
gone on consecutive long-distance tours

there is only the literal
concrete mass of living
escaped meaning
paints my soul of pallor
and disregard for giving

too real
reality when existential
lacking import
life no more essential

the unveiling leaves only an abutment of "why"
unanswerable without a figurative reply

laughter is a good thing

no worries
time flows
the list ticks off

i'll not be finished
when death visits

choice

oh this blistering maze
of choice filled days
my indecisive ways
set my mind ablaze
a fog or permanent glaze

there's a dark one

no space for connecting
a chasm separates our light
that dark domain between
vacuums that steel their way to steal our life

no ease when chest feels to burst
gasps for ... for ... for what
it's fear that lies
lying in wait
always perpetrator of fake news

cast in shadows of past calamity
imaginings of tomorrow's apocalypse
it is fear that raises voice
disguised as fury
anger not the culprit but the protective projectile

the arrow meant to slay
before the beast within can be revealed
we suffer loss and misdirection
entombment the imagined remedy

scared stiff
paralytic rage the ointment
but like a mummy shroud
wraps our once thriving life-force
now hidden by fear's lie triumphant

security

maybe it's my age
that i be looking for securit ... oops
almost said that evil word
that stifles creative angst
slits the throat of the artist's voice
squeezes by the balls
squelching possibility and conception

phooey fa fa
boo ... hisssssssssssssssssssssssss

life
we get older
older
not bolderrrrrrrrrrrr

been looking for time to stop the unstoppable
momentum g-force on overdrive
out of control

ah ... chaos
the rest all an illusion

so
visit the ocean blue
smell the saltwater
drink port with the neighbors

till 3:00 in the morning
crash in a blur
wake up to a good cup of brew
do it all over again

life
so short and sweet
with some dill on the side
remnants of good sherry
afterglow of passionate fuck'n'
lover gone
didn't get a name
the life of small
little homo sapiens

piss in the streets
fireworks on the horizon
ballgame victory win

just time enough
to die or live
die among the living
or live among the dying

just time enough
just time

time

grandest illusion of all
time

let's find her underbelly
penetrate the viscous vixen
there's only confusion here
the warm comforting
blanket of no sense

the reality
within the real

only one then it's done

like a snowflake
a sand grain
a star 'n'
drop o' rain

like a blizzard
or a beach
cosmos 'n'
hurricane

the many make one
the ones make many
unique yet plenty

and you
individual
and yet
universal

only one
gifts your own
for all to receive
you've just to believe

only one
then it's done

season of free

where's this remembered
season of free
these childish eyes
this vision to see
everything new
always a first
in time gave way
to unquenchable thirst
the light of childhood
to darkness within

where's the vigor
of youth's idealism been
missing in action
'cos of pain's tempering wind
gales of loss
forged the sheltering wall
latter days' mourning's
fill the heart's hallowed hall
its silver and gold
tarnished and black

a light in this night
just even a crack
so from these trials
to momentarily distract
an inward beacon
a child's innocence reclaimed
childhood's end
no longer be blamed
resignation or recognition
still choosing to be

perhaps recapture
the season of free
before life's forces
take pleasure to flee
once more heart's brilliance
a luminous burst
to shine in this life
before spirit's dispersed
its super nova expansion
to join the universe

awoke

4:00 am
an air of grief
having lost mom

beyond belief
she is not in phone call reach

missing her laughing
telling her stories

missing seeing her
those twinkling eyes

so 4:00 am
sitting quietly
remembering

sweet to do so

i forget i can locate them still
here in my middle
where ache and emptiness play

in that middle where
excavation has opened again
mom and dad
sanctuaried within

grief II

stabbing pain
heartache's lament
how oft must i receive thee
unwelcome
perennial guest
upon my doorstep

longtime acquaintance
not by design or desire

reluctant playmates are we

Section II

Grief Takes a Holiday

autumnal romance

oh this sheltered season of the heart
ablaze in autumn sumac blush
finds still
love's fires raging

the present tide of numinous wonder and mystery

all is revealed in a single grain of silica under foot
in the gazed upon star of cobalt heavens
within the folds of fern leaf
unfurled splendor bathed in solar caress
coaxing to stretch and yawn
its way to a new dawn

all is revealed in a single breath
slowly drawn filling sinew and bone
molecular energetic aspiration
the ins and outs of breathing
spent in the duty of sacred continuance
the organism so bent on its existence

all is revealed in the little excavations
cut through life's meandering losses
presence of the lost and no longer present
daily gift the unremembered
closing unexpected groundbreaking of heart
reminder of those who inevitably depart

all is revealed in the eyes of the beloved
undressed exposure to a lover's knowing
revealed in the experiences
that live in the silence between echoes
that unspeakable beyond-words energy
that calls each one to her destiny

in the hold of her embrace

awakening to the gift of a new autumn dawn
the sunburst blast of migration departing sky-born wings
i find my heart consumed with longings for nature
a few years to be with the earth
not concrete urban petrification
people-buzzing insignificance
natural pure communion with our terran parent

in the midst of this desire i am not alone

hand in mine there you are
your eyes a molecular bonding gaze
into the heart of me

we are children together
in love
my sister bride friend
in the hold of her embrace

haiku4u

my chest feels to burst
i am floating in orbit
your eyes capture me

in the wind today

i sensed your caress in the wind today
our body-subtle quivers
in the shimmering foliage of the trees

how magnificent the sky
with fluid floating cloud mist
re-membering for me
the drape and flow of
your brown beauty mane
upon my pillow

like fields saturated with clover
i am filled with an abundance of blossoming emotion
whispered in the bouquet of sweet magnolia
pollinating my breathing
with the essence of you

how marvelously made
arachnid spun web of care and nurturing
i found it in the needles of pine today

not unlike your fingers
delicate as the tiniest violet veins
moving upon ebony
graceful as that spider's spinning

you and i
spinning a web of deep communion
an intersecting pause
of heart-scape repose

first kiss

empty - now
the feeling within my center
as night imposes its domain
time piece noted
earth mom completes another spin
since your last eve's departure

candle luminosity
ignites memories of your night light arrival
i relive joyfully
our walk under star lit frosted sky
conversing as we stray and tentatively embrace
laughing at cat paw patter
following the distressed mew
of our four-footed companion

the three of us
kitchen arrival to raisin apple warmth
feast on the earth born nectar
and me
i seek your luminary eyes
arriving at the threshold of your affections
i am touched in some forgotten realm of inner tranquility
warmed and excited

having hesitated too long
proclamation of our desire
as if to savor
the vertigo of passion's gyre

words slowly whispered
"i want to kiss you"

as lips softly touch
flesh generates the passion
this first kiss's blush
of lust's fires are fashioned

seed-self of glory

swelled in saturation
rain cleansed earth yields to sprouts unseen
the wake of winter's steed

hidden promise
buried eves ago
presses hard against the surface
weakening crust of inhibition

seed-self of glory
struggling strength
breaks into the light
a cloudburst of knowing

drinking drinking drinking

ride on

thinking of my need for self-reflection
these weeks of autumn sumac blush
the beauty of fire painted arbor
i sit to write again

i love this season in the north
all of nature whispering ides of change
delicious undeniable truth
not long i arrive forty years hence my birth

life is a winged mare of exceptional speed
i shall grasp her mane
riding her ways to the breadth of my days

oh that she might run long and far
before my weakened grasp
loosens its grip

ride on ride on

rebirth

floating within your moist dark beauty
i find a newly discovered heart beating within my own
as if always two hearted i've roamed

i was despair
until this moment

opening my eyes
it is as if their first opening

and here you are
on the outside
heart beating
and me believing again

carnal awakening

i love you goddess
light your bodice
illuminating heart
to my day's start

to touch your skin
texture of satin
your body warm
a sensual storm

her eyes

it is her eyes that find entry to my soul

to know her is to love her
to love her is to encounter the celestial graces
to forsake all for one more glance into the depth of her
mysteries

her body
poetry of cosmic motion
her arms and legs
timeless movement of the spheres

her scent the bouquet of a rain soaked desert
her touch the embrace of a god's lover

her breasts
the contours of her belly
the lines of her hips and buttocks
like the sands of Zanzibar
ever shifting
shape changing
like the beating wings of Eros she writhes
in the arms of love's pleasures

her kiss is the touch of the tiniest spring flower
seeking expression amidst late winter snow
the decay of fallen autumn

and her sex
her sex tastes of the seas
salt of the earth
citrus of eden

but it is her eyes that find entry to my soul

a lover's touch

your every cell that sings its siren song
lulls my flesh further along

encouraging its pulse in rhythm to your breathing
chests in heated passion recover from rapid beating

the lust that grows from our head to our toes
the mane that flows across your pillows

these memories as such
remnants of a lover's touch

stair-steps of love

it starts
  with a whispered glance
    promise of new romance
      kiss of ignition flame
        without threat of sin or blame
      a certain knowing
        love starts flowing
        newly awakened
          to flower full bloom
        newly awakened
        love starts flowing
      a certain knowing
        without threat of sin or blame
      kiss of ignition flame
    promise of new romance
  with a whispered glance
it starts

the impact of you

blue skies
sea foam surf
crisp eucalyptus air scent
green needled pine
mountain view beauty

my breathing in of creation

but you

as the dew graces the berry
sunlight the meadow forested glen
moonlight the high Sierras

make me more

as it is

my heart excited
washing my soul
sweet impressions of you
i cannot stop the sluice gate from flowing

i want your touch
your sacred trust
the eye to eye rush
of love's mysteries much

not to mention the lust

cycle

in the small wondering
in the gift of loving
in being loved
there lies deep meaning

the true wonder
despite apparent losses
love spent
eclipsed by the leaving lover
for the love of another

i find myself risking
love again

chanson de rêve (dream song)

... and when the ocean
gives up her light
she darkens
a little less bright

touching the sky
with a new prick of glimmer
she transfers the bright
to the sea foam's shimmer

fished from the wave crests
adrift on the shore
placed by dear Lucia
to shine evermore

sons of the sea
cobalt blanket of night
carries their own
bioluminescence of white

... and when the ocean
gives up her light
humans their dreams
these stars ignite

premier rêve – rêves des rêveurs (first dream –
dream of dreamers)

if i were to dream dreamers dreaming
i would dream dreamers dreaming
of my own dreams of dreaming
and in those dreams of dreamers dreaming
of my own dreams of dreaming

i would be dreaming
of all the things
that dreamers dream

deuxième réve – la lune
(second dream – the moon)

i am the moon
dead world
ancient dust

scarred orb
tethered gray white
to a living world
of silver-blue light

visage received from a distant sun
for limited nights
then for a time
the visage is done

i am distance
its chasm to span
between two points of light

i am infinity
breadth of comprehension
to confound mind's sight

i am a vacant sea
of monster creatures
that once ruled the night

i am receiver of the human dreamers'
footprints of presence upon my dust
though from my surface
human presence has rushed

upon my reflection
silvery white
the human dreamer
peers deep into night
ancient dreamer
through modern science's light

we are the same stuff
these humans and me
star stuff of gas
nebula and sea

makings of galaxies
our celestial array
same stuff of the universe
that's how we play

it's my tethered visage
gives rise in the day
inspiring night's dreaming
to inspire their way

vivian

what a kit this cat
comes fully assembled
some parts disposable
hairball regurgitation the least desirable

white mittens rise
paws coloring to gray striped leggings
pursed white triangle snout
cheshire grin in profile

what a kit this cat
piece of work
expectant 5:00 am mews
demanding she is for her pre-dawn fête

chasing my tracks to bedroom
no effort leap
headfirst curl onto her side
stretched out body awaiting massage

what a kit this cat
orphan upon the steps
our newly purchased home
interloper now resident

vertical glistening eyes
hide her sly device
give just enough to seduce
claim her title entitled

what a kit this cat
comes fully assembled
no part disposable
hairball regurgitation now deigned tolerable

|•

Section III

Word Shadows

Genesis

Always, I have been fascinated by the quickness and speed of cats. Often, I have been totally arrested by that oh so familiar crouch of a stalking feline. The hungry intensity in her eyes, as she burns her gaze on the subject of her sight, the startling side to side body shift beginning in the hind quarters, quickening fur tracing spine to head, alert with focused anticipation. The cat's contemplation of making game of its prey. The quick dart of a blurred phantom image, sprung upon the unsuspecting guest. A Pounce, Bounce, dribble game of high jump tease and it's over. Stillness ... Disinterested in the lack of action, trophy left behind, the feline preens with tongue-soaked fur-sponge in the warmth of a new sun ... satisfied in deed.

I was nine years old, at best. I had been playing in the front yard on a beautiful spring day. The air crisp with the fresh cut grass of a first spring mowing. Like the day, everything was fresh, new. The trees were almost fully budding, tulips popping throughout my view. I lay in the fresh cut clippings listening to the sounds of my neighborhood. I could hear my father in the garage cleaning the lawn mower blade, plotting its next archrival conquest. I heard the sound of the Kirby vacuum as it sucked away the tainted dust entrapped in the shag of the living room carpet, ready receptacle of defiling soil once again. I closed my eyes. My hearing more acute in this sun-drenched eye-lid pseudo darkness cast in peach-pink hues, I stretched to hear everything: the wind as it caressed my fallen body, the hum of a passing plane as it distanced into faint memories of other passings — all passings blending into one with the smells, the spring-cast light fall — an archetypal memory of all of my nine springs born again, in innocence. I knew this place, this setting, this moment, this peace. I knew this place as my home.

I opened my eyes, sat up and beheld with fascination. A newly arrived robin was pecking up seed-gift left by my father. Smokey, our cat, sat in crouched intensity, observing, summoning decision. Slowly she stalked sloth-like a few inches closer, side shifted her hips and, WHOOSH! A blur of gray, levitated off the ground, the pounce, a shriek of inhuman whistle, and my eyes followed the graceful yet speedy brown V-like animation of the robin as it passed overhead, safely out of reach of an invisible cat-trap snare. I looked at Smokey in time to catch an appealing stare matched by the cry of a proud but disappointed hunter.

Moments later found the robin returned to its feast, the cat eyeing it wantonly from a distance. If only the cat could fly! I decided to help. Modeling its stealth, I picked up the cat and slowly stole toward the feeding prey. I was no longer. My body, hands holding the cat created the extension. My spirit, my sight, my movement, my prey was one with the cat. All vision left me except for the bobbing, darting body of brown-feathered fluff. The cat, too, saw nothing else as it became intently focused on this once lost chased-ling. Amazement must have filled the hunter as it glided airborne by its conspiring catapult to land deftly upon its object. No pounce, no bounce, no dribble-game of high-jump tease. Just stillness ...

I stared at the lifeless bird. I couldn't fathom the quickness, the stealth, the immediacy of the loss. The bird was dead. I stared at the lifeless bird. My father had seen it all. Rushing to stop the chase, arriving, deed done. I stared at the lifeless bird.

Dad was yelling something at me and chased the cat away. I was being taken into the house, away from the sweet-grass scent of my archetypal spring, hastened to my room, denied the grandeur of the remaining day. I lay on my bed, eyes closed, bewildered, confused. In my mind's eye, all I could do was stare at the lifeless bird.

No more sounds, no more smells, no more spring, all things changed, no longer home.

Musings of a Touring Artist

What is it that drives my passion anyway? What truly makes me tick? Am I driven by the realization that death will finally come, ending all the life and experiences I enjoy? Will my consciousness be ultimately obliterated in my passing? At times, I think it must be, yet I truly do not know. In fact, the truth is that I don't really know what drives my passion, my love for living.

It is difficult to be on this life journey, especially when here, touring alone, making so many contacts, and none at a truly intimate level. I am left to confront the deep hollow absence in the core of the "me" I seldom take time to "be" with.

What is the value of all this travel and meetings of others? What do I have of real significance to say to anyone I do not know deeply? Do I know anyone deeply in the first place? Do I have anything of significance to say, for that matter, to anyone? Perhaps I should just be listening ...

... here's a thought! "All things end."

You know, when I really listen, often that is what I hear most resoundingly! "All things end." Perhaps it is endings that we are obsessed with, we humans. I think I am. I am always haunted by a past ending, with so much of my present choices based on an experience, long ended; captive of a past "me", trapped in a present "me" that always longs for a future "me" that will be the literal death of "me". I am my own destiny!! In the end "I" and "me" will be one and the same. And who will know me? Who will pause to even think of me?

Yet, with all these questions I continue, not without pain, not without loneliness, not without passion, to choose from a multitude of possibilities, forging a future I can scarcely glance, making my way to some final future, the future that ultimately brings the radical end of "me".

Passionately, on I go to meet my death, personal, singular, a brief moment in the life of the universe. In some sense, then, I am barely a life, less than a single lightning bolt, a mere whimper in a cacophony of swirling stuff, galactic gyre, mass and matter, only to drift toward what? Toward endlessness? Infinity?

It makes me wonder, "Who the hell do I think I am?"

|•

After Word

beyond horizon

in the distance beyond horizon
to the gods of my own standing
i surrender

heresy

expansion of the minimal truths
presented to us in our early years'

faith systems

onset
higher levels of awareness
spiritual growth

we cannot help but become heretical
going beyond early learning

my heresy
embraced
expanded from
Roman Catholic tutelage

if soul exists at all
it must
equally
energize all of creation

not just creatures
but the very fabric
of the cosmos
the universe
right down to
the tiniest of particles
space and even time itself

if soul
then ubiquitous soul
or none at all

animals
insects
flora and fauna
the seas and the sands
the planets
the galaxies
and should they exist
plentitude of universes

the whole of it
energized by mystery
something

all of it
all of human experience
that which we identify as good
as evil
that which we deem worthy
and of little value
all of it

and of it all
we humans
at our best
animated by love

the most challenging
of all heresies

to dare to love

especially

ourselves

litany for humanity

what if we are all the same person
what if we are all the same
what if we are all
what if we are
what if we
what if
what
what if
what if we
what if we are
what if we are all
what if we are all the same
what if we are all the same person

then we're all tired
then we're all energized
then we're all depressed
then we're all sad
then we're all burdened
then we're all joy filled
then we're all celebrating
then we're all despairing
then we're all imagining
then we're all creative
then we're all destructive
then we're all pleasant & kind

then we're all belligerent and hateful
then we're all loving
then we're all Christ & the Buddha
then we're all the devil & the demon
then we're all defensive
then we're all vulnerable
then we're all open
then we're all receptive
then we're all considerate
then we're all selfless
then we're all selfish
then we're all despising
then we're all talented
then we're all dull
then we're all impatient
then we're all mindful
then we're all biased
then we're all racist
then we're all dead
then we're all alive
then we're all funny
then we're all appealing
then we're all attractive
then we're all undesirable
then we're all needing
then we're all fulfilled
then we're all angry
then we're all anxious
then we're all devastated

then we're all resilient
then we're all disenfranchised
then we're all at home
then we're all worn thin
then we're all at war
then we're all peacemakers
then we're all non-binary
then we're all enlightened
then we're all in the dark
then we're all afraid
then we're all courageous
then we're all frantic
then we're all peaceful

then *we* are *all*

| •

CPSIA information can be obtained
at www.ICGtesting.com
Printed in the USA
BVHW010411210922
647580BV00013B/17/J

9 798986 404912